This book is dedicated to our daughters
Dwayna, Tyhela, Laylah and Danielle

Creole Entrée - a New Orleans style of cooking that is a highly seasoned food ususally prepared with rice, okra, tomatoes, peppers and seafood which makes use of chopped celery, bell peppers and onions from Cajun cooking but has a variety of European, French and African influences. The African influence, which was extensive, came about because nearly all servants were African-American, as were many of the cooks in restaurants and cafes.

MAMA DOWN THE BAYOU

RECIPES WITH

SHOPPING LIST

Or

A cookbook on how to plan a holiday party, family celebration, event or special occasion with Southern and Creole Cajun recipes, timelines and shopping lists

MAMA DOWN THE BAYOU

RECIPES WITH

SHOPPING LIST

THOU Management

Publishing Dept

Post Office Box 913

Conley, Ga. 30288

Edition ISBNs   978-0-9820080-0-3

Library of Congress Control Number: 2008906690

Library of Congress Subject Headings:

Cookery, American-Louisiana Style

Cookery, Cajun

Cookery, Creole

First Edition 2008

Cover Photography by

Tobias Smith Photography

Pictureman533@aol.com

1.0

TABLE OF CONTENTS

ABOUT THE AUTHORS

Vera Richardson, Barbara Whittington and Yvette Fairley-Scott get together every year with their mother Lillian Batiste to plan, shop, prep food and cook for the holidays and on other special occasions. It has become a tradition over the years to follow this format which has helped them to become more organized and save time. They are originally from Louisiana but Vera, Barbara and Yvette now reside in Atlanta, Georgia's metropolitan area.

ACKNOWLEDGEMENTS

Lillian Batiste:
I thank God for all my children especially Vera, Barbara & Yvette for putting this book together. God has blessed me with seven children and I thank Him. I also give thanks to God for my husband, Lionel Batiste, for his support and sticking with me. For this cause I bow my knees unto the Father of our Lord Jesus Christ of whom the whole family of heaven and earth is named; without God in my life I can do nothing. 1 Cor 3:13

Vera Richardson:
Special thanks to my family and friends; especially Wilbert Richardson, Sr., Dwayna & Ricky Lockhart, Sr., Ariana Johnson and Tyhela Whittington for all the good memories with time spent while helping to test these recipes. Thanks to my partners Barbara and Yvette, who without your help I could have never pulled this off. Thanks for sticking in there when this vision seemed bigger than us. And thanks mom for passing on these treasured loving recipes. This book somehow has helped me to go back and be thankful for my grandmother who we so dearly called "Mama down the bayou". She passed these recipes on to my mother, who passed it on to me and my sisters and now we have passed this on to our daughters. I don't think my grandmother knew that with everything changing around her that one thing would stay constant, her recipes; this is *her-story* being passed from mother to daughter. It has linked our daughters, who never had the pleasure to know her loving spirit, back to our grandmother. Now while testing and successfully recreating these entrées, there in their eyes is this gleam; they now know her spirit. My hope and prayer is that this book uplifts you somehow and brings your families together near and far. To God be the Glory always...Love you more!

Barbara Whittington:
This book is in dedication to my heirs, TJ and Tyhela Whittington, the manifestation of God's favor in my life.

To "Mama down the bayou" who gave love unconditionally to all her grandchildren.

To my mother who worked diligently in the kitchen preparing home cooked meals for all of us.

And last but not least to God the Father, God the Son and God the Holy Ghost; my life, my love, my legacy.

Yvette Fairley-Scott:
I would like to thank God;
who made this book possible.

To thank my sisters;
who made this journey worth while.

To my family who made this book necessary;
and to my mother who made this dream a reality.

WARNING-DISCLAIMER

This book is designed to provide information on cooking Southern Creole recipes. It is sold with the understanding that the publisher and authors are not engaged in professional cooking.

It is not the purpose of this book to know everything about food allergies or be responsible for improper preparation, event planning, and food prices but instead to make available to families an optional way to organize and prepare for special occasions.

Every effort has been made to make this book as complete and accurate as possible. However, there may be mistakes, both typographical and in content. Therefore, this text should be used only as a general method and not as the ultimate source for Southern Creole cooking and event planning. Furthermore this book contains information on food prices that is current for Georgia and Louisiana as of Dec 2007.

The purpose of this book is to help families organize and entertain. The author and THOU Management – Publishing Dept shall have neither liability nor responsibility to any person or entity with respect to any loss or damage caused, or alleged to have been caused, directly or indirectly, by the directions and/or recipes contained in this book.

If you do not wish to bond by the above, you may choose not to purchase this book.

How to Use this Book

This book is designed for planning an event with pre-selected Southern Creole entrées for family and friends for about thirty-five to forty people. It should be used as a guide to help you organize and save time planning this menu for your special event. It is assumed that all entrées will be used so the menu has already been divided up for six families to purchase and prepare. Of course if you have less than or more than 6 families, you can divide the entrées between the families as appropriate. Schedule your meetings, elect an organizer and choose a family member to represent each family as the POC (Point-Of-Contact). Assign each family to an entrée and/or action item and record your decisions in the space provided at the end of each chapter. There are also extra pages to add your family favorite entrées and blank pages at the end of each chapter to record notes. After each meeting, distribute the meeting notes to the assigned POC (Point-Of-Contact).

There are prep recipes for a lot of the entrées. It is highly recommended that you use the Prep Recipes which will help you save time on the day of the event. After using the Prep Recipes, go to Chapter 7 to resume the recipe at the point denoted by the two asterisks **. Cayenne Red Pepper is used in this cookbook to spice up the recipes and if omitted will not take away from the flavor of the entrée. Also included are my grandmother's favorite two recipes, fried bread and succotash. Most recipes can be halved and even a third for a family size serving. There are calendars in Appendix III you can use to help schedule meetings and action items. Remember ovens and ranges may vary, so you may need to change the recommended temperature or heat levels.

Sauté - to cook food quickly in a small amount of oil in a skillet or sauté pan over direct heat.

First Meeting - Selecting the Menu

Decide which family's house is central to all family members to have all your meetings. This way you won't have too many members traveling too far to attend the meetings and there will be no confusions of where the meetings are held. Schedule a date and time for your first meeting at least one month and half before the event to discuss the menu.

First choose an event organizer to keep the meetings focused, record meeting notes and notify the families or POC (Point-Of-Contact) the results after each meeting. Second, decide the location of the family event. By choosing the location this will determine which family is the host family. The host family is either the family member whose house the event will take place or has the connection to secure the location. Also the eve of event dinner will be served by the host family as everyone gathers to help prepare the event menu, setup and decorations. A good host location would be the family that has a big kitchen for all the cooking and prep work that will take place. Third, decide on the menu for both the event and eve of event. A good idea is to ask everyone present what is their favorite dish or family activity for this occasion and try to accommodate. This will help other family members feel they are a part of the planning. Also decide on a small menu for the eve of the event. Many of you will have to get together the day before the event to complete the prep work and/or setup and decorate. Fourth, choose a POC person from each family and record their email addresses. And lastly schedule a date and time for the next family meeting. Now, you have decided on the family meeting house, the host family, the event organizer family member and the family member POC. So the next step is to decide on the menu. Below you will find the pre-selected Southern Creole dishes for your event and space provided to add other favorite entrées of your own family. Try to spread these responsibilities around as much as possible so everyone will enjoy the pleasure of planning a successful event. Fill in the space provided below on the decisions you have made thus far. Also remember to record the meeting notes and distribute to the POC for each family.

Fill in the space provided below:

Meeting Date: _____ Time: _____

Meetings Location: _____

Event Organizer: _____

Event Location: _____

Event Date: _____ Time: _____

Host Family: _____

Family 1 POC: _____
Email Address: _____

Family 2 POC: _____
Email Address: _____

Family 3 POC: _____
Email Address: _____

Family 4 POC: _____
Email Address: _____

Family 5 POC: _____
Email Address: _____

Family 6 POC: _____
Email Address: _____

Next Meeting Date: _____ Time: _____

Select menu from the entrées below.

Event Menu			
Gumbo			Cornbread Dressing
Ham			Strawberry Shortcake
Sweet Peas			Stewed Mirliton
Turkey			Mustard Greens
Baked Spaghetti Cheese Casserole			Baked Stewed Chicken
Dirty Rice Shrimp Etoufffe'			Stewed Okra Crawfish Etouffee'
Stuffed Bell Peppers			Wheat Dinner Rolls
Sweet Potato Pie			Coconut Pie
			Coconut Pecan Pie
Yams			Peach Cobbler
Pecan Pie	.		Homemade Candy
Bread Pudding			Potato Salad
Apple Pie			Rum Sauce
Ice Cream			Drinks

Miscellaneous and Family Activities			
Plastic ware			**Aluminum Pans&Foil**
Napkins			
Paper Towels			**Ice Chest**
			Ice
Games			**Music & Dances**
Newly Wed Game			Music (DJ and/or CD's)
Family Feud			Cupid Shuffle
Card Games			Bus Stop/Electric Slide
Charade			Soul Train Line
Dominoes			
Transport Out of Town Guests		Priceless	**Decorations**

Select your eve of event menu from the entrées below:

Eve of the Event Menu			
Lasagna			**Red Beans & Rice**
Eggnog			**Homemade Candy**
Teacakes			

Record family favorite entrées in the space provided below:

Family Favorite Entrées			

Record meeting notes and distribute to POC:

Meeting Date: _____   Time: _____

_____

_____

_____

_____

_____

_____

_____

_____

_____

_____

_____

_____

_____

_____

_____

_____

_____

_____

_____

_____

_____

_____

_____

_____

_____

_____

_____

_____

_____

_____

_____

_____

Cajun Trinity - Onions, bell peppers and celery, the three most often used ingredients in Cajun/Creole cooking.

Second Meeting – Listing Entrée Ingredients

Schedule this meeting at least three weeks or more before the event. The purpose of this meeting is to create the grocery list of ingredients for each entrée you have chosen and confirm any decisions that needed to be made in previous meetings. On the next page are the Southern Creole dishes and their grocery list of ingredients. Seasonings and other common ingredients for all entrées were put in its own category to avoid duplication of effort. The music, dance and games category are only suggestions and is intended for all families to contribute to the event. Remember to include more seasonings if you have added any of your favorite recipes. In addition there is space provided to add your favorite entrées list of ingredients. Again record the meeting notes and distribute to each family POC.

Grocery list of ingredients for each entrée/group:

Event Menu Grocery List			
Gumbo			**Cornbread Dressing**
Gizzard			Corn meal
Bologna			Self-rising Flour
Chicken Wings			Eggs
Crabs			Medium Raw Shrimp
Raw Shrimp			Dried Shrimp
Smoked Turkey Necks			Whole Milk
Andouille and Smoked Sausage			**Coconut Pecan Pie**
Dried shrimp			Ready Made Pie Crust
Oysters			Pecans
Okra			Honey
Tripe			Cornstarch
Gravy Packs			Coconut
Ham			
Ham			**Stewed Mirliton**
Brown Sugar			Mirliton
Slice Pineapples			Raw Shrimp
Cinnamon			Dried Shrimp (small)
Toothpicks			Canola Oil
Turkey			
6 lbs Turkey			**Mustard Greens**
Gravy Mix			Mustard Greens
Baked Stewed Chicken			Smoke Turkey Necks
Wings/Legs/Thighs			Jalapeños
Gravy Packs			Canola Oil

Shrimp Etouffee'			Crawfish Etouffee'
Raw Shrimp			Crawfish Tails
Vegetable Oil			Vegetable Oil
Creole Instant Roux Mix			Creole Instant Roux Mix
Cayenne Red Pepper			Cayenne Red Pepper
Homemade Crust /Teacakes			**Baked Spaghetti Cheese Casserole**
Yellow Cake Mix			Margarine
Flour			Pasteurized Cheese Block
Sugar			Dry Cheese Packs
Margarine			Evaporated Milk
Nutmeg			Four Shredded Cheese Pack
Eggs			American Slice Cheese
Vanilla			Spaghetti
Dirty Rice			**Potato Salad**
Rice			Potatoes
Creole Instant Roux			Eggs
Turkey Ground			Mayo
Ground Beef			Mustard
Cream of Mushroom Soup			Sweet Relish
Cream of Chicken Soup			Sandwich Spread
Raw Turkey Sausage			Black Pepper
Beef Broth			Salt

Stuffed Bell Peppers			Stewed Okra	
Whole Bell Peppers			Okra	
Raw Shrimp			Raw Shrimp	
Bread Crumbs			Andouille Sausage	
Jalapeños			Cayenne Red Pepper	
			Dried Shrimp	
Sweet Peas			Canola Oil	
Sweet Peas				
Margarine				
Sweet Potato Pie			**Coconut Pie**	
Sweet Potatoes			Coconut	
Sugar			Nutmeg	
Eggs			Milk	
Margarine			Cornstarch	
Vanilla Extract			Eggs	
Nutmeg			Margarine	
Cinnamon			Vanilla	
Homemade Crust Recipe			Homemade Crust Recipe	
Yams			**Peach Cobbler**	
Sweet Potatoes			Peaches	
Sugar Substitute Brown Sugar			Cornstarch	
Sugar Substitute White Sugar			Margarine	
Margarine			Sugar	
Vanilla			Homemade Crust Recipe	

Homemade Candy			Pecan Pie		
Condensed Milk			Ready Made Pie Crust		
Sugar			Pecans		
Margarine			Honey		
Peanut Butter			Margarine		
Pecans			Cornstarch		
			Sugar-Free Brown Sugar		
			Cinnamon		
Bread Pudding			**Apple Pie**		
Bread (Wheat/White)			Upside Down Crumb Pie (store bought)		
Raisins					
Crush Pineapples			**Strawberry Shortcake**		
Coconut(optional)			Strawberries (Fresh or Frozen)		
Sugar/Sugar-Free			Whip Cream		
Whole Milk			Yellow Cake Mix		
Eggs			Vanilla		
Vanilla			Strawberry Sauce		
Margarine					
Cinnamon			**Bread Pudding Rum Sauce**		
Dark Rum			Dark Rum		
			Brown Sugar		
Wheat Dinner Rolls			Vanilla		
Dinner Rolls			Margarine		
			Evaporated Milk		
Ice Cream					
Neapolitan					

Miscellaneous and Family Activities

Plastic ware			Decorations		
Cups					
Plates					
Bowls					
Napkins					
Paper Towels			Aluminum Foil & Pans		
			7 Large Pans		
Drinks & Ice			10 Medium Pans		
Sprite/Coke/Orange Soda			1 Large Foil Roll		
Ice Chest			1 Small Foil Roll		
Ice					
Games			Music & Dances		
Newly Wed Game			Music (DJ and/or CD's)		
Family Feud			Cupid Shuffle		
Card Game			Bus Stop/Electric Slide		
Charade			Soul Train Line		
Dominoes					
Transport Out of Town Guests		Priceless			

List ingredients for each eve of the event entrée:

Eve of the Event Menu			
Lasagna			**Red Beans & Rice**
Lasagna Noodles			Red Beans
Spaghetti Sauce			Smoke Turkey Wings
Turkey Ground			Smoke Sausage
Ground Beef			Cayenne Red Pepper
Three Cheese Shredded Mix Pack			Canola Oil
American Slice Cheese			Rice
Tomato Paste			*Seasonings*
Sharp Shredded Cheddar Cheese			Mexican Unique Seasonings
Canola Oil			All Purpose Seasoning
			Mince Garlic
Eggnog			Yellow Onion
Whole Milk			Shallots (Green Onion)
Eggs			Bell Peppers
Sugar			Parsley
Evaporated Milk			Cilantro
Whiskey			Creole Seasoning
Nutmeg			Season All
			Creole Instant Roux Mix
			Bay Leaves
			Filet' Gumbo Mix

List ingredients for each Family Favorite entrée:

Family Favorite Entrées			

Record Meeting Notes and distribute to POC:
Meeting Date: _____ Time: _____

_____

_____

_____

_____

_____

_____

_____

_____

_____

_____

_____

_____

_____

_____

_____

_____

_____

_____

_____

_____

_____

_____

_____

_____

_____

_____

_____

_____

_____

_____

_____

Al dente – a term used for cooking pasta; cooked enough to be firm but not soft.

3

Third Meeting - Pricing and Delegating Entrées

Your third meeting should be schedule at least two weeks before the event. The purpose of this meeting is to get an estimated price of each entrée; a grand total of the amount needed for the event and delegate the entrées evenly between the families. First, price each ingredient to get a total for each entrée or group and record the total in the $$ column. Second, total all entrées and get a grand total for the event rounded up to the nearest hundred. Then divide the number of families by the grand total to get each family's contribution amount.

For example,
    Five families
    Event Grand Total = $496.00 rounded up to $500.00
    Each Family's Contribution = $100.00

On the next several pages are the Southern Creole dishes already divided up for six families (i.e. Family 1, Family 2, Family 3…). Now allow each POC to choose a number that will correspond to their family. If their total purchases exceed the family contribution you may need to move one or two entrées to another family. Priority items are based on entrées that can be prepped in advance and should be purchased one week before the event and delivered to the host family location for preparation and storage. Schedule all other items to be delivered to the host family location two days before the event. In the table below quantities are specified in standard and metric measurements and are separated by a slash. Common ingredients have been grouped together to avoid duplication of effort like the Seasoning group. See an example of pricing in Appendix 1. Also there is space provided to add your favorite entrées list of ingredients and pricing. Confirm your family activities, decorations, the event date, time and location. Remember to record the meeting notes and distribute to each POC.

Record your decisions in the spaces provided below:

Meeting Date: _____ Time: _____

Number of Families: _____

Event Grand Total: _____

Each Family Contribution Amount: _____

Priority Items Due Date: _____

All Other Items Due Date: _____

Specify below which family is assigned to Family 1, Family 2, Family 3 and Family4 and so on...

Family 1 is _____

Family 2 is _____

Family 3 is _____

Family 4 is _____

Family 5 is _____

Family 6 is _____

Eve of the Event Dinner and Preparation:

Location: _____

Date: _____ Time: _____

Confirm Family Activities:

Confirm Event Date: _____ Time: _____

Next Meeting Date: _____ Time: _____

Price each entrée and designate a number to each family:

Event Dinner Menu Grocery List					
Gumbo	**Family 2**	**$$**	**Cornbread Dressing**	**Family 3**	**$$**
Gizzard	2.5 lbs/ 1.1k g		Corn Meal	2 lbs/ 907 g	
Bologna	1 lb/ 454 g		Self-rising Flour	2 lbs/ 907 g	
Chicken Wings	5 lbs/ 2 kg		Eggs	4	
Crabs	1 dz.		Med Raw Shrimp	2 lbs/ 907 g	
Raw Shrimp	3 lbs/ 1.4k g		Dried Shrimp	1 pk.	
Smoke Turkey Necks	5 lbs/ 2.26 kg		Whole Milk	Half qt/ 473 ml	
Andouille and Smoke Sausage	1.5lb ea. /680 g ea.				
Dried Shrimp	2 – 3 pk.				
Oysters	Small Jar				
Okra	5 lbs/ 2.26 kg				
Tripe	1 pk.				
Creole Instant Roux Mix	4 Cans				

Ham	Family 5	$$	Potato Salad	Family 4	$$
Ham	4 lbs/ 1.81 kg		Potatoes	5 lbs/ 2.26 kg	
Brown Sugar	Small Bag		Eggs	1 dz	
Slice Pineapples	1 Can		Mayo	Large	
Cinnamon	Small		Mustard	Med. Jar	
Toothpicks	Small		Sweet Relish	Med. Jar	
			Black Pepper	Small	
Wheat Dinner Rolls	Family 4	$$	Sandwich Spread	Small Jar	
Rolls	40-45		Salt	Small	
			Parsley	Small	
Stewed Mirliton	Family 5	$$	Relish	Small	
Dried Shrimp	1 Small pk.		**Baked Stewed Chicken**	Family 4	$$
Raw Shrimp	2lbs/ 907g		Wings,Legs& Thighs	10 lbs/ 5kg	
Mirliton	12 count		Creole Instant Roux Mix	Small Can	
Canola Oil	Small				

Turkey	Family 4	$$	Mustard Greens	Family 3	$$
Turkey	6 lbs/ 2.7kg		Mustard Greens	12 Bunches or Bags	
Creole Instant Roux Mix	Small Can		Smoke Turkey Necks	1.5 lbs/ 680g	
			Jalapeños	1 Large	
			Canola Oil	Small	
Baked Spaghetti Cheese Casserole	**Family 2**	**$$**	**Sweet Peas**	**Family 4**	**$$**
Margarine	2 sticks		Margarine	1 pk.	
Pasteurized Cheese Block	2lbs block box		Sweet Peas	6 lbs/ 2.7kg	
Dry Cheese Packs	3 pk.		**Crawfish Etouffee'**	**Family 3**	**$$**
Evaporated Milk	32 oz/ 907g		Crawfish Tails	36 oz/ 1kg	
Four Shredded Cheese Pack	8 oz/ 227g		Creole Instant Roux Mix	1 Can	
American Slice Cheese	1 lb/ 454g		Vegetable oil	1 Small Bottle	
Spaghetti	2 lbs/ 907g		Cayenne Red Pepper	Small	

Dirty Rice	Family 6	$$	Stewed Okra	Family 1	$$
Rice	3 lbs/ 1.4 kg		Okra	6 lbs/ 2.7 kg	
Creole Instant Roux Mix	1 Small Can		Raw Shrimp	3 lbs/ 1.4 kg	
Turkey Ground	2 lbs/ 907 g		Andouille Sausage	3 lbs/ 1.4 kg	
Ground Beef	2 lbs/ 907 g		Cayenne Red Pepper	1 Bottle	
Cream of Mushroom Soup	1 Can		Dried Shrimp	Small pk	
Cream of Chicken Soup	1 Can		Canola Oil	1 qt/ 1 l	
Raw Turkey Sausage	½ lb/ 225g		**Shrimp Etouffee'**	**Family 4**	**$$**
Beef Broth	Med.		Raw Shrimp	3 lbs/ 1.4 kg	
			Creole Instant Roux Mix	1 Can	
			Cayenne Red Pepper	Small	
			Vegetable Oil	Small Bottle	
			Jalapeños	1 Large	

Sweet Potato Pie	Family 1	$$	Coconut Pie	Family 3	$$
Sweet Potatoes	5 lbs/ 2.26 kg		Coconut	14 oz/ 396g	
Sugar	Small Bag		Nutmeg	Small	
Eggs	4		Milk	Small	
Margarine	2 Sticks		Cornstarch	Small	
Vanilla Extract	Small		Eggs	2	
Nutmeg	Small		Margarine	1 Stick	
Cinnamon	Small		Vanilla	Small	
Homemade Crust	See Recipe		Homemade Crust	See Recipe	

Yams	Family 1	$$	Peach Cobbler	Family 1	$$
Sweet Potatoes	5 lbs/ 2.26 kg		Peaches	6 lbs/ 2.7kg	
Sugar-Free Brown Sugar	Small Bag		Cornstarch	Small Package	
Sugar-Free White Sugar	Small Bag		Sugar	Small Package	
Margarine	1 Stick		Margarine	1 Stick	
Vanilla	Small		Homemade Crust	See Recipe	

Pecan Pie	Family 3	$$	Homemade Candy	Family 3	$$
Ready Made Pie Crust	2		Condensed Milk	8 cans	
Pecans	12 oz/ 340g		Sugar	10 lbs/ 5kg	
Honey	12 oz/ 340g		Peanut Butter	Small	
Margarine	1 Stick		Margarine	1 Stick	
Cornstarch	Small		Pecans	1 pk.	
Sugar-Free Brown Sugar	Small				
Cinnamon	Small				

Stuffed Bell Peppers	Family 4	$$	Bread Pudding Rum Sauce	Family 4	$$
Whole Bell Peppers	10		Dark Rum	Small	
Raw Shrimp	2 lbs/ 907g		Brown Sugar	14 oz/ 396g	
Bread Crumbs	Small		Vanilla	Small	
Jalapeños	1		Margarine	1 Stick	

Store Bought Items	Family 5	$$	Bread Pudding	Family 4	$$
Sprite,Coke, Orange Soda	45 Cans		Raisins	1 Large Box	
Assorted Kids Drinks	24 pk.		Crush Pineapples	1 Large Can	
Bottled Water	24 Bottles		Bread	1 loaf	
Upside Down Apple Pie	1		Coconut	16 oz/ 454 g	
Neapolitan Ice Cream	1 Gal/ 3.78 l		Sugar/ Sugar-Free	16 oz/ 454 g	
			Whole Milk	1 qt/1 l	
Strawberry Shortcake	**Family 4**	**$$**	Eggs	4	
Strawberries (Fresh or Frozen)	1 Pint/ 0.5 l		Vanilla	Small	
Whip cream	16 oz/ 454 g		Margarine	1 Stick	
Yellow Cake Mix	1 Box		Cinnamon	Small	
Vanilla	Small		Dark Rum	Small	
Strawberry Sauce	1 Pack				

Eve of the Event Dinner Menu					
Lasagna	**Family 1**	**$$**	**Red Beans & Rice**	**Family 6**	**$$**
Lasagna Noodles	1 lb/454g		Smoke Sausage	1 lb/454 g	
Spaghetti Sauce	2 Jars (Regular)		Smoke Turkey Wings	1 lb/454 g	
Turkey Ground	2 lbs/ 907g		Red Beans	2 lbs/ 907g	
Ground Beef	2 lbs/ 907g		Canola Oil	Small Bottle	
Three Cheese Shredded Mix Pack	1 pk.		Cayenne Red Pepper	Small Bottle	
American Slice Cheese	24 pk.		Rice	Large Bag	
Sharp Shredded Cheddar Cheese	1 pk.		**Eggnog**	**Family 4**	**$$**
Tomato Paste	12 oz/ 340g		Whole Milk	½ gal/ 1.89 l	
Canola Oil	Small		Eggs	1 dz	
			Sugar	Small Bag	
			Evaporate Milk	2 Cans	

Miscellaneous					
Plastic ware	Family 1	**$$**	**Music & Dance**	**All Families**	**$$**
Cups	100 Count		CD's		
Plates	100 Count		Cupid Shuffle		
Bowls	100 Count		Bus Stop		
Napkins	250 Count		Soul Train Line		
Paper Towels	2 Large Pk		Electric Slide		
Spoons	100 Count				
Games	**All Families**	**$$**	**Ice**	**All Families**	**$$**
Newly Wed Game			Ice Chest	1 per family	
Family Feud			Ice	1 per family	
Card Games					
Charade					

Seasoning	Family 6	$$	Home made Crust	Family 5	$$
Mexican Unique Seasonings	2 boxes		Cake Mix	4 boxes	
All Purpose Seasoning	2 cans		Flour	10 lbs/ 5kg	
Mince Garlic	1 jar		Sugar	5 lbs/ 2.26 kg	
Yellow Onion	2 bags		Margari ne	4 sticks	
Shallots (Green Onion)	4 bunches		Eggs	8	
Bell Peppers	10 large				
Parsley	2 bunches				
Cilantro	1 bunch				
Creole Seasoning	2 cans				
Season All	1 can				
Bay Leaves	1 pk				
Filet' Gumbo Mix	1 jar				

Aluminum Foil & Pans	Family 1	$$
7 Large Pans		
10 Medium Pans		
1 Large Foil Roll		
1 Small Foil Roll		
Transport Out of Town Guests	Priceless	

Specify below which family is assigned to the Prep Items and deliver to host family by due date:

Prep Items	Assigned To	Delivery Date
Coconut Pie Filling		
Sweet Potato Pie Filling		
Raw Shrimp Peeled and De-veined		
Chop Fresh Seasoning		
Prep Stuffed Bell Peppers		
Prep Dirty Rice		
Prep Turkey		
Prep Stewed Baked Chicken		
Prep Mustard Greens		
Prep Stewed Mirliton (Chayote Squash)		
Prep Gumbo Ingredients		
Prep Lasagna		

Specify below which family is assigned to the Family Favorite Prep Items and deliver to host family by due date:

Family Favorite Prep Entrées	Assigned To	Delivery Date

List ingredients for your family's favorites:

Family Favorite Entrées			

Record Meeting Notes and distribute to POC:
Meeting Date: _____ Time: _____

_____
_____
_____
_____
_____
_____
_____
_____
_____
_____
_____
_____
_____
_____
_____
_____
_____
_____
_____
_____
_____
_____
_____
_____
_____
_____
_____
_____
_____
_____

4

Prep Recipes

All POC's should meet at the host family location to complete all prep entrées in advance one week before the event. This will help you save time on the day of the event. Prep entrées should be stored at the host family location in freezer safe bags or containers. Cayenne Red Pepper is used to spice up these recipes and if omitted will not take away from the flavor of the entrée. A good tip is to measure and set aside all your ingredients before starting your recipe. Below are the preparation steps.

1. All raw shrimp should be peeled, de-veined and placed in freezer bag. Shrimp shells should be placed in a separate freezer bag. Store items in freezer until the eve of the event.

2. All fresh seasoning can be chopped in food processor which is listed below. Use some of the fresh seasoning for the Prep Recipes in this chapter and place remaining in separate freezer bags and store in freezer until the eve of the event.

Prep Fresh Seasoning
Yellow Onion
Shallots (Green Onion)
Parsley
Bell Peppers

3. Ingredients for the dirty rice sauce mixture should be prepared and frozen.

Prep Dirty Rice

Standard	Ingredients	Metric
3 cups	Creole Instant Roux	0.7 l
2 lbs	Ground Turkey	900 g
2 lbs	Ground Beef	900 g
8 oz.	Cream of Mushroom Soup	227 g
8 oz.	Cream of Chicken Soup	227 g
1½ cup	Beef Broth	375 ml
2 tsp	Season All	9.9 ml
2 tsp	Creole Seasoning	9.9 ml
2 tsp	Mexican Unique Seasonings	9.9 ml
2 tsp	All Purpose Seasoning	9.9 ml
4 tsp	Mince Garlic	19.7 ml
1 cup	Yellow Onion	236.6 ml
1/3 cup	Shallots (Green Onion)	78.9 ml
3 tbsp	Parsley	44.4 ml
1/3 cup	Bell peppers	78.9 ml

Mix Creole instant roux in medium bowl according to package to create amount of roux needed and set a side. Place ground beef and ground turkey in a medium sauce pan over medium heat and cook until slightly brown. Drain grease from meat. Return sauce pan to low heat with drained meat and add season all, Creole seasoning, mexican unique seasonings, all purpose seasoning, mince garlic, yellow onion, shallots (green onion), parsley and bell peppers. Cook for 10 minutes over medium low heat. Add beef broth, roux, cream of mushroom and cream of chicken soup to sauce pan. Cook for 30 minutes on medium - low heat stirring occasionally. Remove from heat and allow cooling.

Place in freezer proof container and store in freezer until the eve of the event.

4. Homemade crust for peach cobbler, coconut pie, sweet potato pie and tea cakes should be prepared and frozen.

Prep Homemade Crust:

Standard	Ingredients	Metric
4	Boxes Yellow Cake Mix	4
10 cups	Flour	2.4 l
2 cups	Sugar	473.2 ml
2 cups	Margarine	473.2 ml
¼ cup	Nutmeg	59.2 ml
8	Eggs	8
¼ cup	Vanilla Extract	59.2 ml
½ cup	Cold water	118.3 ml
	Cooking Spray	

Melt margarine in microwave and set aside. Pour cake mix in large bowl. Add melted margarine, sugar, nutmeg, eggs, vanilla extract and cold water in a large bowl. Slowly add a third of flour and mix thoroughly. Slowly add another third of flour and mix again. Now add remaining flour and knead until it becomes into a consistency of dough. Place half of the dough in freezer safe bag and store in freezer until the night before the event. Refrigerate other half of dough for 20 minutes. Base three pie baking dishes with cooking spray. Flatten dough with rolling pin to line the three pie baking dishes. Remove excess dough from rim and flatten remaining dough with rolling pin and cut into 24 strips to use later for the coconut and sweet potato pies.

5. Coconut and sweet potato pies should be prepared and frozen.

Prep Coconut Filling:

Standard	Ingredients	Metric
14 oz	Coconut	396g
1 tsp	Nut Meg	4.93 ml
½ cup	Milk	118.3 ml
1 tbsp	Cornstarch	14.79 ml
2	Eggs	2
¼ cup	Margarine	59.2 ml
1 tsp	Vanilla	4.93 ml
2 tbsp	Water	29.6 ml
	Cooking Spray	

In a medium sauce pan add margarine, milk, nutmeg, vanilla, cornstarch and water on medium heat for 5 minutes or until mixture thickens (do not allow mixture to boil). Remove from heat and set aside. Mix eggs and add to mixture. Stir in coconut. Pour filling into homemade crust created in preparation step number 4. Evenly place 4 strips horizontally and 4 vertically over filling. Let cool, place in freezer proof container and store in freezer until the eve of the event.

Prep Sweet Potato Filling:

Standard	Ingredients	Metric
5 lbs	Sweet Potatoes	2.26 kg
2 ½ cup	Sugar	591.5 ml
4	Eggs	4
1 cup	Margarine	236.6 ml
2 tsp	Vanilla Extract	9.9 ml
½ tsp	Nutmeg	2.46 ml
1 tsp	Cinnamon	4.93 ml
½ cup	Flour	118.3 ml
	Cooking Spray	

(Makes 2 pies)

Rinse sweet potatoes and place in large pot with enough water to cover sweet potatoes and boil for 1 ½ hours or until tender. Strain water from sweet potatoes and rinse with cold water and set aside until sweet potatoes are cool to the touch. Peel and then mash sweet potatoes and margarine in a large bowl. Add flour, nutmeg, vanilla, sugar and mix thoroughly. Pour filling into homemade crust created in preparation step number 4. Evenly place 4 strips horizontally and 4 vertically over filling. Let cool, place in freezer proof container and store in freezer until the eve of the event.

6. Okra should be fried, drained and frozen

Prep Stewed Okra

Standard	Ingredients	Metric
6 lbs	Cut Up Okra	2.7 kg
1 qt	Canola Oil	1 l

Place oil and okra in a large sauce pan. Fry okra for 45 minutes or until lightly brown. Drain oil from okra. Let cool, place in freezer proof container and store in freezer until the eve of the event. If you selected this entrée for your event, also do Prep Steps 1 and 2 with this Prep Recipe; refer to recipes in Chapter 7 for the exact amount.

7. Stewed Baked Chicken should be seasoned and frozen.

Prep Baked Stewed Chicken

Standard	Ingredients	Metric
10 lbs	Chicken (thawed)	5 kg
2 tsp	Season All	9.9 ml
2 tsp	Creole Seasoning	9.9 ml
2 tsp	Mexican Unique Seasoning	9.9 ml
2 tsp	All Purpose Seasoning	9.9 ml

Combine season all, Creole seasoning, mexican unique seasonings, all purpose seasoning in a small bowl. Sprinkle season mixture evenly over chicken. Place in freezer proof container and store in freezer until the eve of the event. If you selected this entrée for your event, also do Prep Step 1 with this Prep Recipe; refer to recipes in Chapter 7 for the exact amount.

8. Turkey should be seasoned and frozen.

Prep Turkey

Standard	Ingredients	Metric
6 lbs	Turkey	2.7 kg
2 tsp	Season All	9.9 ml
2 tsp	Creole Seasoning	9.9 ml
2 tsp	Mexican Unique Seasonings	9.9 ml
2 tsp	All Purpose Seasoning	9.9 ml
1 tsp	Mince Garlic	4.93 ml
¾ cup	Yellow Onion	177.6 ml
¼ cup	Shallots (Green Onion)	59.2 ml
2 tbsp	Parsley	29.6 ml
¼ cup	Bell peppers	59.2 ml

Combine season all, Creole seasoning, mexican unique seasonings and all purpose seasoning in a small bowl. Rub season mixture over entire turkey including cavity. Mix yellow onion, shallots (green onion), parsley, bell peppers and add mince garlic in a small bowl. Stuff fresh seasoning created in preparation step number 2 inside turkey cavity. Place in freezer bag and store in freezer until the eve of the event.

9. Lasagna should be prepared and frozen.

Prep Lasagna

Standard	Ingredients	Metric
2	Jars Spaghetti Sauce (Regular Size)	2
2 lbs	Turkey Ground	900 g
2 lbs	Ground Beef	900 g
1	Pack Three Cheese Mix	1
1	Pack Slice Cheese (24 Count)	1
1 pk	Sharp Shredded Cheddar Cheese	1
12 oz	Tomato Paste	340 g
½ tsp	Season All	2.46 ml
½ tsp	Creole Seasoning	2.46 ml
½ tsp	Mexican unique seasonings	2.46 ml
½ tsp	All Purpose Seasoning	2.46 ml
1 tsp	Mince Garlic	4.93 ml
1 cup	Yellow Onion	236.6 ml
1/3 cup	Shallots (Green Onion)	78.9 ml
1/3 cup	Parsley	78.9 ml
1/3 cup	Bell peppers	78.9 ml
1 tbsp	Oil	14.79 ml
1 lb	Lasagna Noodles	454 g
	Baking Spray	

Boil lasagna noodles according to package and set aside. Place ground beef and turkey ground in large sauce pan on medium heat until lightly brown. Drain excessive oil if necessary and return to medium heat. Add season all, Creole seasoning, mexican unique seasonings, all purpose seasoning, mince garlic, yellow onion, shallots (green onion), parsley, and bell peppers. Add spaghetti sauce and tomato paste and let cook for 5 minutes and set aside. Base lasagna pan with baking spray and place enough meat sauce in lasagna pan to cover entire pan. Layer noodles on top and cut to fit the length of the pan; add another layer of meat sauce to cover noodles then layer cheeses on top. Repeat process until pan is almost full ending with noodles. Pour remaining meat sauce and sprinkle with remaining cheeses. Let cool and store in freezer until the eve of the event.

10. Mirliton (Coyote Squash) should be boiled whole, peeled, cut into quarters and then frozen.

Prep Stewed Mirliton

Standard	Ingredients	Metric
12	Mirliton (Coyote Squash)	12

Thoroughly rinse mirliton and place in a large pot with enough water to cover mirlitons. Boil mirliton for 1 ½ hours. Strain water from mirlitons and rinse with cold water and set aside until mirlitons are cool to the touch. Peel mirlitons and remove core. Dice into cubes and place in freezer proof container and store in freezer until the eve of the event. If you selected this entrée for your event, also do Prep Steps 1 and 2 with this Prep Recipe; refer to recipes in Chapter 7 for the exact amount.

11. Stuffed bell peppers should be prepared and frozen.

Prep Stuffed Bell Peppers

Standard	Ingredients	Metric
10	Whole Bell Peppers	10
2 lbs	Raw Shrimp	900 g
2 cups	Bread Crumbs	473.2 ml
1 tsp	Season All	4.93 ml
1 tsp	Creole Seasoning	4.93 ml
1 tsp	Mexican Unique Seasonings	4.93 ml
1 tsp	All Purpose Seasoning	4.93 ml
1 tsp	Mince Garlic	4.93 ml
1 cup	Yellow Onion	236.6 ml
1/3 cup	Shallots (Green Onion)	78.9 ml
1/3 cup	Parsley	78.9 ml
1/3 cup	Bell peppers	78.9 ml
4 tbsp	Margarine	59.2 ml
½ cup	Dried shrimp	118.3 ml
1	Large Jalapeño Pepper	1
1 cup	Shrimp Stock	236.6 ml

Dice yellow onion, shallots (green onion), parsley, and bell peppers and set aside. Peel and de-vein raw shrimp and set aside; place shrimp shell in large pot of water and boil for 30 minutes. Strain liquid from shrimp shells to create shrimp stock; discard shells and set shrimp stock aside. Remove insides of jalapeños, dice into small pieces and set a side. Place dried shrimp in warm water and set a side. Remove stem from bell peppers, cut in half and discard inside of bell peppers. Fill large pot with water; place on high heat and bring water to a boil. Add halved bell peppers to boiling water for 4 minutes. Remove halved bell peppers from water and place in baking dish. Melt margarine in a large sauce pan and sauté mince garlic, yellow onion, shallots (green onion), parsley, bell peppers for 3 minutes on medium heat. Add raw shrimp, dried shrimp, season all, Creole seasoning, mexican unique seasonings, all purpose seasoning, jalapeños and shrimp stock and cook for 2 minutes on medium high. Remove from heat and add bread crumbs and mix thoroughly. Stuff filling into each halved bell pepper shell. Let cool, place in freezer proof container and store in freezer until the eve of the event.

12. Ingredients for gumbo should be prepared and frozen.

Prep Gumbo

Standard	Ingredients	Metric
1 lb	Whole Bologna	454 g
5 lbs	Chicken wings	2.26 kg
12	Frozen or Live Blue Crabs	12
1.5 lb	Andouille Sausage	680g
1.5 lb	Smoke Beef Sausage	680g
1	Pack of Tripe	1
½ tsp	Season All	2.46 ml
½ tsp	Creole Seasoning	2.46 ml
½ tsp	Mexican Unique Seasonings	2.46 ml
½ tsp	All Purpose Seasoning	2.46 ml
5 lbs	Cut Up Okra	2.26 kg
1 qt	Canola Oil	1 l

Combine season all, Creole seasoning, mexican unique seasonings and all purpose seasoning in a small bowl. Rinse chicken and sprinkle season mixture over chicken. Slice sausages and chop bologna into bite size cubes. For live crabs, run hot water over live crabs for 15 minutes or until crabs are no longer moving. After crabs have cooled, clean crabs by removing membrane and break in half. Cut tripe in small squares. Place oil and okra in a large sauce pan. Fry okra for 45 minutes or until lightly brown. Drain oil from okra. Place each ingredient in separate freezer proof container and store in freezer until the eve of the event. If you selected this entrée for your event, also do Prep Steps 1 and 2 with this Prep Recipe; refer to recipes in Chapter 7 for the exact amount.

13. Mustard greens should be boiled with smoked turkey necks and then frozen.

Prep Mustard Greens

Standard	Ingredients	Metric
12	Bunches Fresh Mustard Greens or Bags Prewashed Mustard Greens	12
1.5 lbs	Smoked Turkey Necks	680 g

Separate mustard leaf from stem and tear into medium pieces. Place in large colander and rinse thoroughly several times until all debris is removed. Boil mustard greens and turkey necks in large pot on medium-high heat for 1 hour. Let cool, drain water, place in freezer proof container and store in freezer until the eve of the event.

14. Record Prep Recipes of your family's favorite:

_____

_____

_____

_____

_____

_____

_____

_____

_____

_____

_____

_____

_____

_____

_____

_____

_____

_____

_____

_____

_____

_____

_____

_____

_____

_____

_____

_____

_____

_____

_____

_____

_____

5

Eve of the Event Dinner and Preparations

It is now the eve of the event. Everyone should be at the host family location and ready to finish the last of the preparations. If you were following the prep recipes in Chapter 3, you should have the eve of event menu ready to prepare to feed everyone who has come to help. All recipes are located in Chapter 7 and Chapter 8 including the recipes to complete the eve of event menu. Below is the eve of the event menu and extra space if you have additional items to serve. The host has been assigned to prepare and serve the eve of the event dinner. Assign others to complete each of the preparation items below.

Eve of the Event Menu			
Lasagna			**Red Beans & Rice**
Homemade Candy			**Eggnog**
Teacakes			

Preparation items are listed below and refrigerate all food items upon completion:
1. Bake coconut and sweet potato pies
2. Prepare and bake pecan pie
3. Prepare and bake bread pudding
4. Prepare and bake coconut pecan pie

5. Prepare and bake corn bread according to package for cornbread dressing
6. Place smoked turkey necks, tripe and gizzards in large gumbo pot with enough water to cover; boil for two hours and allow to cool
7. Remove all previously prepared frozen items and place in kitchen sink to thaw for the event
8. Bake yellow cake according to package for strawberry shortcake
9. Cook rice according to package for dirty rice
10. Decorate location for event (if applicable)

Additional space for prep items to complete your family's favorite recipes:

_____
_____
_____
_____
_____
_____
_____
_____
_____
_____
_____
_____
_____
_____
_____
_____
_____
_____
_____

6

The Event Schedule

The day has finally come for the celebration. Below is a schedule you can follow to complete the event menu. Assuming you have used the Prep Recipes, the list below gives you an idea of what to start preparing and a time line to prepare them. See Chapter 7 and 8 for all recipes. There is also space provided to list additional items you may have added to complete for your event. Check off each item as you complete them. Remember to add your family's favorite entrées to this list.

9:00 am Place the following entrées in the oven:
- o   Turkey
- o   Based Ham
- o   Baked Stewed Chicken
- o   Stuffed Bell Peppers
- o   Additional Event Items:

_____

_____

9:30 am Begin cooking the following entrées:
- o   Mustard Greens
- o   Stewed Okra
- o   Stewed Mirliton
- o   Baked Spaghetti Cheese Casserole
- o   Large pot of rice for other entrées
- o   Additional Event Items:

_____

_____

10:30 am Start preparing the following entrées:
- o Cornbread Dressing
- o Gumbo
- o Potato Salad
- o Yams
- o Shrimp Etouffee'
- o Crawfish Etouffee'
- o Additional Event Items:

_____

_____

11:30 am Reheat and/or prepare the following entrées
- o Dirty Rice
- o Sweet Peas
- o Pecan Pie
- o Coconut Pecan Pie
- o Bread Pudding
- o Peach Cobbler
- o Additional Event Items:

_____

_____

12:00 pm Complete the following items
- o Reheat all other pies at 350°F/180°C for 10 minutes or until pies reach 110°F/43°C for serving
- o Heat wheat dinner rolls
- o Finish strawberry shortcake
- o Start setting up buffet
- o Additional Event Items:

_____

_____

1:00 pm Begin the event
- o Gather family for prayer
- o Serve and enjoy
- o Additional Event Items:

_____

_____

_____

_____

_____

_____

_____

_____

_____

_____

_____

_____

Roux – A gravy base for most Creole soups, sauces and entrées. A mixture of equal parts flour and oil cooked together and used as a thickening.

7
Entrée Recipes

This chapter contains the recipes for the Southern Creole entrées. Keep in mind if you have prepared any of the prep recipes then you have completed part of the recipe. Two asterisks ** denote the starting point to complete the entrée. Some recipes have suggestions and/or tips. The recipes also contain both standard and metric measurements and are separated by a slash. Cayenne Red Pepper is used to spice up these recipes and if omitted will not take away from the flavor of the entrée. A good tip is to measure and set aside all your ingredients before starting your recipe. There is also space provided at the end of this chapter to add your Family's Favorite Recipes.

Okra Gumbo
(32 Servings)

Standard	Ingredients	Metric
2 tsp	Season All	9.9 ml
2 tsp	Creole Seasoning	9.9 ml
2 tsp	Mexican Unique Seasonings	9.9 ml
2 tsp	All Purpose Seasoning	9.9 ml
5 lbs	Chicken wings	2.26 kg
2.5 lbs	Gizzard	1.1 kg
1	Pack of Tripe	1
5 lbs	Smoke Turkey Necks	2.26 kg
1 pk.	Dried Shrimp	1 pk.
3 lbs	Raw Shrimp	1.4 kg
3 cups	Shrimp Stock	0.7 l
1.5 lb	Andouille Sausage	680g
1.5 lb	Smoke Beef Sausage	680g
1 lb	Whole Bologna	454 g
1 cup	Yellow Onion	236.6 ml
½ cup	Shallots (Green Onion)	118.3 ml
1/3 cup	Parsley	78.9 ml
½ cup	Bell peppers	118.3 ml
12	Frozen/ Live Blue Crabs	12
1 qt	Canola Oil	1 l
5 lbs	Okra	2.26 kg
4 cups	Creole Instant Roux	1 l
1	Small Container Oysters	1
1 tbsp	Cayenne Red Pepper	14.79 ml
1/3 cup	Mince Garlic	78.9 ml
2 tbsp	Gumbo file	29.6 ml
4 gal	Water for Gumbo	15.1 l
	Cooking Spray	

Tip:
Frozen blue crabmeat can be substituted for live crabs.
It is best to use non-stick pots when frying.
This entrée is served with rice so you can start cooking
your rice before starting this recipe.

Preheat oven to 400°F/200°C.
Combine season all, Creole seasoning, mexican unique seasonings and all purpose seasoning in a small bowl. Rinse chicken, place in greased baking pan and sprinkle 2 tsp/9.9 ml of season mixture over chicken. Bake uncovered for 45 minutes or until chicken is lightly brown and set aside. Rinse and discard any fat from gizzards. To start the gumbo mixture; boil tripe, gizzards and turkey necks for 2 hours or until tender in water (check recipe for the amount). **Soak dried shrimp in small bowl and set aside. Peel and de-vein raw shrimp and set aside; place shrimp shells in large pot of water and boil for 30 minutes. Strain liquid from shrimp shells to create shrimp stock; discard shells and set shrimp stock aside. Slice sausages and chop bologna into bite size cubes and set aside. Dice yellow onion, shallots (green onion), parsley, and bell peppers and set aside. For live crabs, run hot water over live crabs for 15 minutes or until crabs are no longer moving. After crabs have cooled, clean crabs by removing membrane, rinse, break in half and set aside. Preheat oil in a large pan and fry okra for 45 minutes until lightly brown. Drain oil from okra, place in strainer and set aside so remaining oil will drain from okra. Mix Creole instant roux mix according to package to create roux and stir into gumbo mixture. Add crabs, sausages, bologna, chicken, dried shrimp, mince garlic, yellow onion, shallots (green onion), parsley, bell peppers, season mixture, shrimp stock to gumbo mixture and return to boil. Add shrimp, cayenne red pepper, oysters and okra. Cook for 5 minutes, remove from heat and add file' to gumbo. Serve in bowl and add cooked rice.

**After using the Prep Recipes in Chapter 4, resume the recipe at this point to complete the entrée.

Ham
(Servings 20)

Standard	Ingredients	Metric
4 lbs	Ham (thawed)	1.81 kg
½ cup	Brown Sugar	118.3 ml
1 Tbsp	Cinnamon	14.79 ml
12 oz	Can Sliced Pineapples	340 g
	Small Box of Toothpicks	

Preheat oven to 350°F/177°C.

Rinse ham, pat dry and place in shallow pan. Pour pineapple juice from canned pineapples in a small bowl and stir in brown sugar; add cinnamon to create glazed mixture. Pour glazed mixture over ham and cover loosely with aluminum foil. Bake for 40 minutes. Remove ham and decorate with pineapples using toothpicks to keep in place. Base ham with glazed mixture within pan and recover with foil. Return to oven and bake for 20 minutes. Ready to serve.

**After using the Prep Recipes in Chapter 4, resume the recipe at this point to complete the entrée.

Baked Stewed Chicken
(16 servings)

Standard	Ingredients	Metric
10 lbs	Chicken (thawed)	5 kg
2 tsp	Season All	9.9 ml
2 tsp	Creole Seasoning	9.9 ml
2 tsp	Mexican Unique Seasonings	9.9 ml
2 tsp	All Purpose Seasoning	9.9 ml
¾cup	Creole Instant Roux	177.6 ml
1 tbsp	Mince Garlic	14.79 ml
1 ½ cup	Sliced Yellow Onion	375 ml
½ cup	Shallots (Green Onion)	118.3 ml
2 tbsp	Parsley	29.6 ml
½ cup	Bell peppers	118.3 ml
	Cooking Spray	

Tip:
Tuck the chicken wings before baking.

Preheat oven to 400°F/200°C.

Dice shallots (green onion), parsley, and bell peppers and set aside. Spray bottom of baking pan. Combine season all, Creole seasoning, mexican unique seasoning and all purpose seasoning in a small bowl and sprinkle season mixture over chicken. **Place chicken in large pan and bake for 45 minutes or until chicken is lightly brown. Remove from oven. Slice onions over baked chicken. Sprinkle mince garlic, shallots (green onion), parsley, and bell peppers over baked chicken. Mix gravy according to package and pour over baked chicken. Place chicken in oven for 30 additional minutes at 425°F /218°C.

**After using the Prep Recipes in Chapter 4, resume the recipe at this point to complete the entrée.

Turkey
(Servings 20)

Standard	Ingredients	Metric
6 lbs	Turkey	2.7 kg
2 tsp	Season All	9.9 ml
2 tsp	Creole Seasoning	9.9 ml
2 tsp	Mexican Unique Seasonings	9.9 ml
2 tsp	All Purpose Seasoning	9.9 ml
1 cup	Gravy Mix	236.6 ml
1 tsp	Mince Garlic	4.93 ml
¾ cup	Yellow Onion	177.6 ml
¼ cup	Shallots (Green Onion)	59.2 ml
2 tbsp	Parsley	29.6 ml
¼ cup	Bell Peppers	59.2 ml

Preheat oven to 400°F/200°C.

Combine season all, Creole seasoning, mexican unique seasonings and all purpose seasoning in a small bowl. Rub season mixture over entire turkey including cavity. Chop yellow onion, shallots (green onion), parsley, bell peppers and add mince garlic in a small bowl. Stuff fresh chopped seasoning mixture inside of turkey cavity. **Place in roaster pan and bake for 1 hour. Remove turkey from oven. Mix gravy according to package and pour over baked turkey. Move stuffed mixture from turkey cavity into roaster pan, base turkey and set oven temperature to 350°F/180°C. Return turkey to oven for 30 minutes or until internal temperature is 165°F/74°C. Ready to serve.

**After using the Prep Recipes in Chapter 4, resume the recipe at this point to complete the entrée.

Baked Spaghetti Cheese Casserole
(Servings 30)

Standard	Ingredients	Metric
2 lbs	Spaghetti	900 g
1 cup	Margarine	236.6 ml
2 lbs	Block Pasteurized Cheese	900 g
3	Packs Powder Cheese	3
1 qt	Evaporated Can Milk	1 l
2 cups	Whole Milk	473.2 ml
8 oz	Four Shredded Cheese Mix	227 g
1 lb	American Slice Cheese	454 g

Tip:
Powder Cheese packets can be found in a box of Mac 'N'
Cheese mix.

Preheat oven to 400°F/200°C.
Boil spaghetti in a large pot according to package, drain and place in large baking casserole dish and set aside. Combine evaporated milk, powder cheese, margarine, slice cheese and block of cheese in large pot, stirring constantly. Cook on medium low heat until all ingredients have melted into a creamy sauce. Pour sauce over spaghetti and mix thoroughly. Add whole milk until mixture is a medium consistency. Place casserole in large pan and sprinkle generously with shredded cheese. Bake for 30 minutes. Remove from oven and let stand for 20 minutes before serving.

**After using the Prep Recipes in Chapter 4, resume the recipe at this point to complete the entrée.

Dirty Rice
(42 servings)

Standard	Ingredients	Metric
6 cups	Rice	1.4 l
3 cups	Creole Instant Roux	0.7 l
2 lbs	Ground Turkey	900 g
2 lbs	Ground Beef	900 g
8 oz.	Cream of Mushroom Soup	227 g
8 oz.	Cream of Chicken Soup	227 g
1½ cup	Beef Broth	375 ml
2 tsp	Season All	9.9 ml
2 tsp	Creole Seasoning	9.9 ml
2 tsp	Mexican Unique Seasonings	9.9 ml
2 tsp	All Purpose Seasoning	9.9 ml
4 tsp	Mince Garlic	19.7 ml
1 cup	Yellow Onion	236.6 ml
1/3 cup	Shallots (Green Onion)	78.9 ml
3 tbsp	Parsley	44.4 ml
1/3 cup	Bell Peppers	78.9 ml

Cook rice according to package. Dice yellow onion, shallots (green onion), parsley, and bell peppers and set aside. Mix Creole instant roux mix in medium bowl according to package to create the amount of roux needed and set a side. Place ground beef and ground turkey in a medium sauce pan over medium heat and cook until slightly brown. Drain grease from meat. Return meat to sauce pan on low heat and add season all, Creole seasoning, mexican unique seasonings, all purpose seasoning, mince garlic, yellow onion, shallots (green onion), parsley, and bell peppers. Cook for 10 minutes over medium low heat. Add beef broth, roux, cream of mushroom and cream of chicken soup to sauce pan and cook for 30 minutes on medium - low heat stirring occasionally. **Mix cooked rice thoroughly to dirty rice sauce and simmer on low heat for 10 minutes. Decorate with parsley and serve.

**After using the Prep Recipes in Chapter 4, resume the recipe at this point to complete the entrée.

Cornbread Dressing
(24 Servings)

Standard	Ingredients	Metric
2 cups	Self-rising Cornmeal Mix	473.2 ml
2 cups	Self-rising Flour	473.2 ml
4	Eggs	4
¾ cup	Margarine	177.6 ml
½ cup	Dried Shrimp	118.3 ml
2 lbs	Medium Raw Shrimp	900 g
½ tsp	Season All	2.46 ml
½ tsp	Creole Seasoning	2.46 ml
½ tsp	Mexican Unique Seasonings	2.46 ml
½ tsp	All Purpose Seasoning	2.46 ml
1 tsp	Mince Garlic	4.93 ml
1 cup	Yellow Onion	236.6 ml
1/3 cup	Shallots (Green Onion)	78.9 ml
1/3 cup	Parsley	78.9 ml
1/3 cup	Bell Peppers	78.9 ml
1 cup	Whole Milk	236.6 ml
7 cups	Shrimp Stock	1.7 l

Preheat oven to 350°F/180°C.

Dice yellow onion, shallots (green onion), parsley, and bell peppers and set aside. Combine flour, cornmeal mix, eggs and milk in a large bowl. Melt ½ cup /118.3 ml of margarine and add to cornbread mixture. Pour batter into greased baking pan. Place in oven and bake for 30 minutes or until golden brown. Remove pan from oven and set aside. Peel and de-vein raw shrimp and set shrimp aside; place shrimp shells in extra large pot of water and boil for 30 minutes. Strain liquid from shrimp shells to create shrimp stock; discard shells and set shrimp stock aside. Melt ¼ cup /59.2 ml of margarine in large pot. Add season all, Creole seasoning, mexican unique seasonings, all purpose seasoning and sauté in mince garlic, yellow onion, shallots (green onion), parsley, and bell peppers for five minutes on medium-low heat. Add shrimp stock, raw shrimp and dried shrimp. Cook on medium heat for 5 minutes. Crumble cornbread into dressing mixture and mix thoroughly. Place in large baking pan and bake for 45 minutes.

**After using the Prep Recipes in Chapter 4, resume the recipe at this point to complete the entrée.

Potato Salad
(32 Servings)

Standard	Ingredients	Metric
5 lbs	Potatoes	2.26 kg
1 dz	Eggs	1 dz
2 ½ cup	Mayonnaise	591.5 ml
4 tbsp	Mustard	59.2 ml
1 cup	Sweet Relish	236.6 ml
2 cups	Sandwich Spread	473.2 ml
1 tsp	Black Pepper	4.93 ml
1 tsp	Salt	4.93 ml
2 tsp	Season All	9.9 ml
2 tsp	Creole Seasoning	9.9 ml
2 tsp	All Purpose Seasoning	9.9 ml
	Parsley (optional)	

Peel potatoes and cut in medium cubes. Place potatoes and eggs in large pot with enough water to cover potatoes and eggs. Boil until potatoes are tender (test by sticking with a fork). Strain water from potatoes and place in large serving bowl. Set eggs aside in separate container in cool water. Mash potatoes until all lumps are dissolved. Peel boiled eggs, set egg whites aside and place yellow yoke in small bowl. Add mustard and ½ cup /118.3 ml of mayonnaise to yoke and mix to create yoke mixture. Slice egg whites into mashed potatoes and add all remaining ingredients; mix thoroughly. Sprinkle dry parsley to decorate and serve.

**After using the Prep Recipes in Chapter 4, resume the recipe at this point to complete the entrée.

Stewed Mirliton (Chayote Squash)
(18 servings)

Standard	Ingredients	Metric
12	Mirliton (Chayote Squash)	12
2 lbs	Raw Shrimp	900 g
½ cup	Dried shrimp	118.3 ml
2 tsp	Season All	9.9 ml
2 tsp	Creole Seasoning	9.9 ml
2 tsp	Mexican Unique Seasonings	9.9 ml
2 tsp	All Purpose Seasoning	9.9 ml
1 tsp	Mince Garlic	4.93 ml
1 cup	Yellow Onion	236.6 ml
1/3 cup	Shallots (Green Onion)	78.9 ml
1/3 cup	Parsley	78.9 ml
1/3 cup	Bell Peppers	78.9 ml
3 Tbsp	Canola Oil	44.4 ml

Tip:
This entrée is served with rice so you can start cooking
your rice before starting this recipe.

Dice yellow onion, shallots (green onion), parsley, and bell peppers and set aside. Place mirliton in large pot with enough water to cover mirlitons and boil for 1.5 hours. Drain water from mirlitons and rinse with cold water and set aside until mirlitons are cool to the touch. Peel skin from mirlitons, discard seed and dice into cubes in a large bowl. Peel and devein raw shrimp and set aside. **Place dried shrimp in cold water and set aside. Place oil in a large sauce pan on medium heat and add mince garlic, yellow onion, shallots (green onion), parsley, and bell peppers and sauté for 5 minutes. Add mirliton in sauce pan and smash. Add dried shrimp, season all, Creole seasoning, mexican unique seasonings, all purpose seasoning to sauce pan and cook on medium heat, stirring occasionally for 30 minutes or until water is absorbed. Add raw shrimp and cook for 5 minutes. Serve over cooked rice.

**After using the Prep Recipes in Chapter 4, resume the recipe at this point to complete the entrée.

Mustard Greens
(Servings 32)

Standard	Ingredients	Metric
12	Bunches Fresh Mustard Greens or Bags of Prewashed Mustard Greens	12
1.5 lbs	Smoke Turkey Necks	680 g
1	Large Jalapeño Peppers	1
¼ cup	Canola Oil	59.2 ml
1 tsp	Season All	4.93 ml
2 tsp	Creole Seasoning	9.9 ml
2 tsp	Mexican Unique Seasonings	9.9 ml
1 tsp	All Purpose Seasoning	4.93 ml

Tip:
You can use two large pots to initially boil the greens and then transfer them to one pot once the mustard greens are tender.
This entrée is served with rice so you can start cooking your rice before starting this recipe.

Separate mustard leaf from stem, tear into medium pieces and discard stems and any discolored leaves. Place in large colander and rinse several times until all debris has been rinsed off. Boil mustard greens and turkey necks in large pot on medium-high heat for 1 hour stirring occasionally. Drain water from mustard greens and turkey necks and return to pot. **Remove insides of jalapeños, dice into small pieces and set a side. Add jalapeno, oil and cook for 15 minutes on medium heat. Add remaining seasoning and cook for another 15 minutes. Serve over cooked rice.

**After using the Prep Recipes in Chapter 4, resume the recipe at this point to complete the entrée.

Stewed Okra
(18 Servings)

Standard	Ingredients	Metric
6 lbs	Cut up Okra	2.7 kg
3 lbs	Raw Shrimp	1.4 kg
3 lbs	Audouille Sausage	1.4 kg
1 cup	Dried Shrimp	236.6 ml
2 tsp	Season All	9.9 ml
2 tsp	Creole Seasoning	9.9 ml
2 tsp	Mexican Unique Seasonings	9.9 ml
2 tsp	All Purpose Seasoning	9.9 ml
½ tsp	Cayenne Red Pepper	2.46 ml
1 tsp	Mince Garlic	4.93 ml
1 cup	Yellow Onion	236.6 ml
1/3 cup	Shallots (Green Onion)	78.9 ml
1/3 cup	Parsley	78.9 ml
1/3 cup	Bell peppers	78.9 ml
1 qt	Canola Oil	1 l
3 cups	Shrimp Stock	0.7 l

Tip:
When frying it is best to use non-stick pots.
This entrée is served with rice so you can start cooking your rice before starting this recipe.

Dice yellow onion, shallots (green onion), parsley, and bell peppers and set aside. Preheat oil in a large pan and fry okra for 45 minutes until lightly brown. Drain oil from okra and set aside in strainer so remaining oil will drain from okra. Peel and de-vein raw shrimp and set raw shrimp aside; **place shrimp shells in large pot of water and boil for 30 minutes. Strain liquid from shrimp shells to create shrimp stock; discard shells and set shrimp stock aside. Slice sausage and set aside. Place dried shrimp in warm water and set a side. Sauté sausage for 5 minutes in an extra large sauce pan on medium low heat. Add mince garlic, yellow onion, shallots (green onion), parsley, bell peppers, season all, Creole seasoning, mexican unique seasonings, all purpose seasoning and cook for 5 minutes. Strain water from dried shrimp. Add shrimp stock, raw shrimp and dried shrimp. Cook on medium heat until raw shrimp turns pink, stirring occasionally. Add okra and let come to a boil for 5 minutes. Serve over cooked rice.

**After using the Prep Recipes in Chapter 4, resume the recipe at this point to complete the entrée.

Stuffed Bell Peppers
(20 Servings)

Standard	Ingredients	Metric
10	Whole Bell Peppers	10
2 lbs	Raw Shrimp	900 g
2 cups	Bread Crumbs	473.2 ml
1 tsp	Season All	4.93 ml
1 tsp	Creole Seasoning	4.93 ml
1 tsp	Mexican Unique Seasonings	4.93 ml
1 tsp	All Purpose Seasoning	4.93 ml
1 tsp	Mince Garlic	4.93 ml
1 cup	Yellow Onion	236.6 ml
1/3 cup	Shallots (Green Onion)	78.9 ml
1/3 cup	Parsley	78.9 ml
1/3 cup	Bell peppers	78.9 ml
4 tbsp	Margarine	59.2 ml
½ cup	Dried Shrimp	118.3 ml
1	Large Jalapeño Pepper	1
1 cup	Shrimp Stock	236.6 ml

Tip:
The same amount of ground beef and/or ground turkey can
be substituted in place of raw shrimp.

Preheat oven to 400°F /200°C.

Dice yellow onion, shallots (green onion), parsley, and bell peppers and set aside. Peel and de-vein raw shrimp and set aside; place shrimp shell in large pot of water and boil for 30 minutes. Strain liquid from shrimp shells to create shrimp stock; discard shells and set shrimp stock aside. Remove insides of jalapeños, dice into small pieces and set a side. Place dried shrimp in warm water and set a side. Remove stem from bell peppers, cut in half and discard inside of bell peppers. Fill large pot with water; place on high heat and bring water to a boil. Add halved bell peppers to boiling water for 4 minutes. Remove halved bell peppers from water and place in baking dish. Melt margarine in a large sauce pan and sauté mince garlic, yellow onion, shallots (green onion), parsley, bell peppers for 3 minutes on medium heat. Add raw shrimp, dried shrimp, season all, Creole seasoning, mexican unique seasonings, all purpose seasoning, jalapeño and shrimp stock and cook for 2 minutes on medium high. Remove from heat and add bread crumbs and mix thoroughly. Stuff filling into each halved bell pepper shell **and bake for 20 minutes. Ready to serve.

**After using the Prep Recipes in Chapter 4, resume the recipe at this point to complete the entrée.

Lasagna
(20 Servings)

Standard	Ingredients	Metric
2	Jars Spaghetti Sauce (regular size)	2
2 lbs	Turkey Ground	900 g
2 lbs	Ground Beef	900 g
1	Pack Three Cheese Mix	1
1	Pack Slice Cheese (24 count)	1
1 pk	Sharp Shredded Cheddar Cheese	1
12 oz	Tomato Paste	340 g
½ tsp	Season All	2.46 ml
½ tsp	Creole Seasoning	2.46 ml
½ tsp	Mexican unique seasonings	2.46 ml
½ tsp	All Purpose Seasoning	2.46 ml
1 tsp	Mince Garlic	4.93 ml
1 cup	Yellow Onion	236.6 ml
1/3 cup	Shallots (Green Onion)	78.9 ml
1/3 cup	Parsley	78.9 ml
1/3 cup	Bell peppers	78.9 ml
1 lb	Lasagna Noodles	454 g
	Baking Spray	

Tip:
Add 1 tbsp/14.79 ml oil when boiling lasagna noodles.
When layering lasagna ensure you save enough meat sauce
for the last layer.

Preheat oven to 400°F /200°C.
Dice yellow onion, shallots (green onion), parsley, and bell peppers
and set aside. Boil lasagna noodles according to package and set aside.
Place ground beef and turkey ground in large sauce pan on medium-
high heat until lightly brown. Drain excessive oil if necessary and
return to medium heat. Add season all, Creole seasoning, mexican
unique seasonings, all purpose seasoning, mince garlic, yellow onion,
shallots (green onion), parsley, and bell peppers. Add spaghetti sauce
and tomato paste and let cook for 5 minutes on medium heat and set
aside. Spray lasagna baking pan with baking spray. Place enough meat
sauce in lasagna pan to cover   bottom of pan. Layer noodles on top
and cut to fit the length of the pan; add sparingly another layer of
meat sauce to cover noodles and then layer three cheese mix, slice
cheese and cheddar cheese on top; repeat process beginning with meat
layer until pan is almost full ending with noodles. Pour remaining
meat sauce and sprinkle with remaining cheeses. **Cover with foil and
bake for 45 minutes. Remove foil and bake for 30 minutes. Allow to
cool before serving.

**After using the Prep Recipes in Chapter 4, resume the recipe at this point to complete the
entrée.

Red Beans & Rice
(15 Servings)

Standard	Ingredients	Metric
2 lbs	Red Beans	900 g
6 cups	Rice	1.4 l
1 lb	Smoke Sausage	454 g
1 lb	Smoke Turkey Wings	454 g
2 tsp	Season All	9.9 ml
2 tsp	Creole Seasoning	9.9 ml
2 tsp	Mexican Unique Seasonings	9.9 ml
2 tsp	All Purpose Seasoning	9.9 ml
1 tsp	Mince Garlic	4.93 ml
1 cup	Yellow Onion	236.6 ml
1/3 cup	Shallots (Green Onion)	78.9 ml
1/3 cup	Parsley	78.9 ml
1/3 cup	Bell Peppers	78.9 ml
¼ cup	Vegetable Oil	59.2 ml
¼ tsp	Cayenne Red Pepper (optional)	1.23 ml

Tip:
For a more Creole dish when serving red beans over cooked
rice add hot sauce.

Cook rice according to package. Rinse beans thoroughly and set aside. Dice yellow onion, shallots (green onion), parsley, and bell peppers and set aside. Fill large pot with 5 quarts/ 4.7 l of water and bring to a boil. Add beans, mince garlic, yellow onion, shallots (green onion), parsley, and bell peppers to boiling water and cook for 45 minutes. Add turkey wings to beans with 1 qt /1 l of water and cook for 30 minutes stirring occasionally ensuring beans do not stick. Add sausage, oil, season all, Creole seasoning, mexican unique seasonings, cayenne red pepper and all purpose seasoning. Cook for 30 minutes on medium low. Serve over cooked rice.

**After using the Prep Recipes in Chapter 4, resume the recipe at this point to complete the entrée.

Crawfish Etouffee'
(14 Servings)

Standard	Ingredients	Metric
36 oz	Frozen Crawfish Tails	1 kg
1 tsp	Mince Garlic	4.93 ml
1 cup	Yellow Onion	236.6 ml
1/3 cup	Shallots (Green Onion)	78.9 ml
1/3 cup	Fresh Parsley	78.9 ml
1/3 cup	Bell peppers	78.9 ml
2 tbsp	Vegetable Oil	29.6 ml
1 tsp	Season All	4.93 ml
2 tsp	Creole Seasoning	9.9 ml
2 tsp	Mexican Unique Seasonings	9.9 ml
1 tsp	All Purpose Seasoning	4.93 ml
3 cups	Creole Instant Roux	0.7 l
¼ tsp	Cayenne Red Pepper	1.23 ml
2 tbsp	Cornstarch	29.6 ml

Tip:
This entrée is served with rice so you can start cooking your rice before starting this recipe.

Mix Creole instant roux mix in medium bowl according to package to create amount of roux needed and set a side. Dice yellow onion, shallots (green onion), parsley, and bell peppers and set aside. Place oil in medium sauce pan and sauté mince garlic, yellow onion, shallots (green onion), parsley, and bell peppers on medium heat for 5 minutes. Add roux, crawfish, season all, Creole seasoning, mexican unique seasonings and all purpose seasoning and bring to a boil. Reduce heat to medium–low and cook for 30 minutes or until crawfish tails are tender. Thoroughly mix cornstarch with 1 tsp/ 4.93 ml of tap water and add to crawfish. Also add cayenne red pepper and cook for 5 minutes. Remove from heat and allow cooling for 5 minutes before serving. Serve over cooked rice.

**After using the Prep Recipes in Chapter 4, resume the recipe at this point to complete the entrée.

Shrimp Etouffee'
(10 Servings)

Standard	Ingredients	Metric
3 lbs	Raw Shrimp	1.4 kg
1 tsp	Mince Garlic	4.93 ml
1 cup	Yellow Onion	236.6 ml
1/3 cup	Shallots (Green Onion)	78.9 ml
1/3 cup	Fresh Parsley	78.9 ml
1/3 cup	Bell Peppers	78.9 ml
2 tbsp	Vegetable Oil	29.6 ml
1 tsp	Season All	4.93 ml
2 tsp	Creole Seasoning	9.9 ml
2 tsp	Mexican Unique Seasonings	9.9 ml
1 tsp	All Purpose Seasoning	4.93 ml
2 cups	Creole Instant Roux	473.2 ml
¼ tsp	Cayenne Red Pepper	1.23 ml
2 cups	Shrimp Stock	473.2 ml

Tip:
This entrée is served with rice so you can start cooking your rice before starting this recipe.

Peel and de-vein raw shrimp and set raw shrimp aside; place shrimp shells in large pot of water and boil for 30 minutes. Strain liquid from shrimp shells to create shrimp stock; discard shells and set shrimp stock aside. Using shrimp stock instead of water, mix Creole instant roux mix in medium bowl according to package to create roux. Dice yellow onion, shallots (green onion), parsley, and bell peppers and set aside. Place oil in medium sauce pan and sauté mince garlic, yellow onion, shallots (green onion), parsley, and bell peppers for 5 minutes. Add roux, season all, Creole seasoning, mexican unique seasonings, all purpose seasoning, mince garlic, yellow onion, shallots (green onion), parsley, and bell peppers to medium sauce pan and bring to a boil. Reduce to medium heat, add raw shrimp and cayenne red pepper and cook for 5 minutes or until raw shrimp turns pink. Remove from heat and allow setting for 5 minutes before serving. Serve over cooked rice.

**After using the Prep Recipes in Chapter 4, resume the recipe at this point to complete the entrée.

Wheat Dinner Rolls
(40 Servings)

Standard	Ingredients	Metric
45	Wheat Dinner Rolls	45

Heat and serve according to package.

Sweet Peas
(28 Servings)

Standard	Ingredients	Metric
6 lbs	Can Sweet Early Peas	2.7 kg
½ cup	Margarine	118.3 ml

Place sweet peas in large pot and add margarine. Cook on medium high for 30 minutes.

Additional space for your family's favorite recipes:

_____

_____

_____

_____

_____

_____

_____

_____

_____

_____

_____

_____

_____

_____

_____

_____

_____

_____

_____

_____

_____

_____

_____

_____

_____

_____

_____

_____

_____

_____

_____

_____

_____

**After using the Prep Recipes in Chapter 4, resume the recipe at this point to complete the entrée.

8

Dessert Recipes

Yams
(Servings 16)

Standard	Ingredients	Metric
5 lbs	Sweet Potatoes	2.26 kg
1 cup	Sugar-Free Brown Sugar	236.6 ml
½ cup	Sugar-Free White Sugar	118.3 ml
½ cup	Margarine	118.3 ml
1½ cup	Water	375 ml
1 tbsp	Vanilla	14.79 ml

Peel and slice potatoes into bowl of cold water. Place potatoes, brown sugar, white sugar, margarine, vanilla and water in large pot on medium heat. Cook for 40 minutes stirring occasionally. Ready to serve.

Sweet Potato Pie
(16 Servings, Makes 2 pies)

Standard	Ingredients	Metric
1	Box Yellow Cake Mix	1
2½ cups	Flour	591.5 ml
½ cup	Sugar	118.3 ml
½ cup	Margarine	118.3 ml
1 tbsp	Nutmeg	14.79 ml
2	Eggs	2
1 tbsp	Vanilla Extract	14.79 ml
2 tbsp	Cold Water	29.6 ml

Homemade Crust:

Spray pie dish with Cooking Spray. Melt margarine. Pour cake mix, melted margarine, sugar, nutmeg, eggs, vanilla extract and cold water in a large bowl. Slowly add half of flour and mix thoroughly. Slowly add remaining flour and knead until it becomes a consistency of dough. Refrigerate for 15 minutes. Divide dough in half. On lightly floured surface with floured rolling pin flatten each halve dough into a circle. Place flatten dough into each baking pie dish and remove excess dough from rim. Flatten remaining dough and cut into 16 one inch strips.

Tip:
You can create tea cakes by using any left over dough of pie recipe; just enough margarine to soften dough.

Standard	Ingredients	Metric
5 lbs	Sweet Potatoes	2.26 kg
2 ½ cup	Sugar	591.5 ml
4	Eggs	4
1 cup	Margarine	236.6 ml
2 tsp	Vanilla Extract	9.9 ml
½ tsp	Nutmeg	2.46 ml
1 tsp	Cinnamon	4.93 ml
½ cup	Flour	118.3 ml
	Cooking Spray	

Sweet Potato Filling:

Preheat oven to 325°F /163°C.
Rinse sweet potatoes and place in large pot with enough water to cover sweet potatoes and boil for 1.5 hours or until tender. Strain water from sweet potatoes and rinse with cold water and set aside until sweet potatoes are cool to the touch. Peel potatoes and then mash sweet potatoes with margarine in a large bowl. Add flour, nutmeg, vanilla, sugar, eggs and mix thoroughly. Gently pour filling to rim of pie crust. Evenly place 4 strips horizontally and 4 vertically over filling. **Bake for 45 minutes. Allow to cool

**After using the Prep Recipes in Chapter 4, resume the recipe at this point to complete the entrée.

Coconut Pie

(Servings 8)

Standard	Ingredients	Metric
1	Box Yellow Cake Mix	1
2½ cups	Flour	591.5 ml
½ cup	Sugar	118.3 ml
½ cup	Margarine	118.3 ml
1 tbsp	Nutmeg	14.79 ml
2	Eggs	2
1 tbsp	Vanilla Extract	14.79 ml
2 tbsp	Cold Water	29.6 ml
	Cooking Spray	

Homemade Crust:

Spray pie dish with Cooking Spray. Melt margarine. Pour cake mix, melted margarine, sugar, nutmeg, eggs, vanilla extract and cold water in a large bowl. Slowly add half of flour and mix thoroughly. Slowly add remaining flour and knead until it becomes a consistency of dough. Refrigerate for 15 minutes. Divide dough in half. On lightly floured surface with floured rolling pin flatten each halve dough into a circle. Place flatten dough into baking pie dish and remove excess dough from rim. Flatten remaining dough and cut into 8 one inch strips.

Tip:
You can create tea cakes by using any left over dough of pie recipe; just enough margarine to soften dough.

Standard	Ingredients	Metric
14 oz	Coconut	396g
1 tsp	Nut Meg	4.93 ml
½ cup	Milk	118.3 ml
1 tbsp	Cornstarch	14.79 ml
2	Eggs	2
¼ cup	Margarine	59.2 ml
1 tsp	Vanilla	4.93 ml
2 tbsp	Water	29.6 ml
	Cooking Spray	

Coconut Filling:

Preheat oven to 350°F /180°C.
In a medium sauce pan add margarine, milk, nutmeg, vanilla, cornstarch and water on medium heat for 5 minutes or until mixture thickens (do not allow mixture to boil). Remove from heat and set aside. Mix eggs and add to mixture. Stir in coconut. Pour filling into pie crust. Flatten remaining dough with rolling pin and cut into 8 strips. Evenly place 4 strips horizontally and 4 vertically over filling. **Bake for 35 minutes.

**After using the Prep Recipes in Chapter 4, resume the recipe at this point to complete the entrée.

Peach Cobbler
(Servings 28)

Standard	Ingredients	Metric
1	Box Yellow Cake Mix	1
2 ½ cups	Flour	591.5 ml
½ cup	Sugar	118.3 ml
½ cup	Margarine	118.3 ml
1 tbsp	Nutmeg	14.79 ml
2	Eggs	2
1 tbsp	Vanilla Extract	15 ml
2 tbsp	Cold Water	29.6 ml

Homemade Crust:

Melt margarine. Pour cake mix, melted margarine, sugar, nutmeg, eggs, vanilla extract and cold water in a large bowl. Slowly add half of flour and mix thoroughly. Slowly add remaining flour and knead until it becomes a consistency of dough. Refrigerate for 15 minutes.

Tip:
You can create tea cakes by using any left over dough of pie recipe; just enough margarine to soften dough.

Standard	Ingredients	Metric
6 lbs	Can Peaches	2.7 kg
½ cup	Cornstarch	118.3 ml
½ cup	Margarine	118.3 ml
1 ½ cup	Sugar	375 ml

Peaches Filling:

Preheat oven to 400°F /200°C.
Cook peaches, margarine and sugar in large pot on medium heat and bring to a boil. Add cornstarch and return to boil and cook for 5 minutes. Remove from heat and let cool. Pour filling into large baking pan. Flatten tennis ball size crust by hand and place over filling. Repeat until entire filling is covered. Place in oven and bake for 45 minutes. Allow to cool and serve with ice cream.

**After using the Prep Recipes in Chapter 4, resume the recipe at this point to complete the entrée.

Pecan Pie
(Serving 16, Makes 2 pies)

Standard	Ingredients	Metric
2	Ready Made Pie Crust (Regular)	2
6 cups	Pecans	1.4 l
12 oz	Honey	340 g
¼ cup	Margarine	59.2 ml
½ cup	Sugar-Free Brown Sugar	118.3 ml
1/3 cup	Light Evaporated Milk	78.9 ml
½ tsp	Cinnamon	2.46 ml
1 ½ tbsp	Cornstarch	22.2 ml

Preheat oven to 375°F /191°C

Melt margarine in medium pot; add honey, sugar, milk, cornstarch, cinnamon and cook on low heat. Add pecans and mix thoroughly. Pour half of filling into each pie crusts. Bake for 20 minutes. Allow to cool and serve.

Coconut Pecan Pie
(Serving 16, Makes 2 pies)

Standard	Ingredients	Metric
2	Ready Made Pie Crust (Regular)	2
6 cups	Pecans	1.4 l
12 oz	Honey	340 g
¼ cup	Margarine	59.2 ml
½ cup	Sugar-Free Brown Sugar	118.3 ml
1/3 cup	Light Evaporated Milk	78.9 ml
½ tsp	Cinnamon	2.46 ml
1 ½ tbsp	Cornstarch	22.2 ml
1 cup	Coconut	236.6 ml

Preheat oven to 375°F /191°C.

Melt margarine in medium pot; add honey, sugar, milk, cornstarch, cinnamon and cook on low heat. Add pecans and coconut and stir thoroughly. Pour half of filling in each pie crust. Place in oven and bake for 20 minutes. Allow to cool and serve.

**After using the Prep Recipes in Chapter 4, resume the recipe at this point to complete the entrée.

Strawberry Shortcake
(24 Servings)

Standard	Ingredients	Metric
1 pint	Fresh or Frozen Strawberries	0.5 l
16 oz	Whip Cream Container	0.5 l
1	Box Yellow Cake Mix	1
1 tbsp	Vanilla	14.79 ml
1	Pack Strawberry Sauce	1

Prepare and bake cake mix according to package. Set aside and allow cakes to completely cool. To create strawberry mixture cut strawberries in half and place in small pot with strawberry sauce. Warm for 3 minutes and set aside to cool. To create whip cream mixture add vanilla to whip cream container and stir thoroughly. Place 1 cake on serving tray upside down and spread whip cream mixture on top. Pour half of strawberry mixture over entire first cake layer. Stack second cake on first cake layer and spread whip cream mixture on top of second layer. Pour remaining strawberry mixture over entire cake. Refrigerate until ready to serve.

Eggnog
(Serving 20)

Standard	Ingredients	Metric
½ gal	Whole Milk	1.89 l
2	Cans evaporated milk	2
12	Eggs	12
3 cups	Sugar	0.7 l
1 cup	Whiskey (optional)	236.6 ml
2 tbsp	Nutmeg	29.6 ml

Tip:
To achieve rich thick foam on top of eggnog, separate the egg whites.

Combine eggs and sugar in a bowl and beat on high until mixture is canary yellow. Stir nutmeg into egg mixture. Combine whole milk and evaporate milk in large pot on medium heat for 30 minutes until warm stirring constantly using a wooden spoon; do not allow milk to come to a boil. Slowly pour 1 cup/236.6 ml of heated milk to bowl of egg mixture and continue to stir. Slowly add egg mixture back into pot while stirring constantly. Remove from heat and stir in whiskey. Ready to serve

---

**After using the Prep Recipes in Chapter 4, resume the recipe at this point to complete the entrée.

Bread Pudding
(Servings 24)

Standard	Ingredients	Metric
2 ¼ cup	Raisins	532.3 ml
1	Loaf Bread	1
1	Can Crushed Pineapples	1
1 qt	Milk	1 l
2 cups	Sugar	473.2 ml
1 cup	Coconut optional	236.6 ml
4	Eggs	4
1 tbsp	Cinnamon	14.79 ml
1 tbsp	Vanilla	14.79 ml
½ cup	Margarine	118.3 ml
1 cup	Dark rum (optional)	236.6 ml
	Cooking Spray	

Bread pudding:

Preheat oven to 350°F /180°C.
Melt margarine and set aside. Tear bread in small pieces into large bowl and pour in milk. Add eggs, sugar, vanilla, cinnamon, pineapples, raisins, coconut, rum and margarine and mix thoroughly. Pour mixture into greased baking dish and bake for 1 hour.

Rum Sauce

Standard	Ingredients	Metric
¼ cup	Dark Rum	59.2 ml
1 cup	Brown Sugar	236.6 ml
1 tsp	Vanilla	4.93 ml
½ cup	Margarine	118.3 ml
½ cup	Evaporate milk	118.3 ml

Melt margarine in a small sauce pan on medium heat. Add milk and brown sugar and allow sugar to dissolve stirring constantly. Remove from heat and add rum and vanilla. Serve sauce over bread pudding.

**After using the Prep Recipes in Chapter 4, resume the recipe at this point to complete the entrée.

Sugar Free Bread Pudding

Standard	Ingredients	Metric
2 cups	Raisins	473.2 ml
1	Loaf Wheat Bread	1
1	Can Crushed Pineapples	1
1 qt	Vanilla Soy Milk	1 l
1 cup	Sugar-Free White Sugar	236.6 ml
1 cup	Honey	236.6 ml
1 cup	Coconut (optional)	236.6 ml
4	Eggs	4
1 tbsp	Cinnamon	14.79 ml
1 tbsp	Vanilla	14.79 ml
½ cup	Margarine	118.3 ml

Bread pudding:

Preheat oven to 350°F /180°C.
Melt margarine and place aside. Tear bread in small pieces into large bowl and pour in milk. Add eggs, sugar, honey, vanilla, cinnamon, pineapple, raisins and margarine and mix thoroughly. Pour mixture into greased baking dish and bake for 35 to 40 minutes.

Rum Sauce

Standard	Ingredients	Metric
¼ cup	Dark Rum	59.2 ml
1 cup	Sugar-Free Brown Sugar	236.6 ml
1 tsp	Vanilla	4.93 ml
½ cup	Light Margarine	118.3 ml
½ cup	Light Evaporate Milk	118.3 ml

Melt margarine in a small sauce pan on medium heat. Add milk and brown sugar and allow sugar to dissolve stirring constantly. Remove from heat and add rum and vanilla. Serve sauce over bread pudding.

**After using the Prep Recipes in Chapter 4, resume the recipe at this point to complete the entrée.

Tea Cakes
(Servings 20)

Standard	Ingredients	Metric
1	Box Yellow Cake Mix	1
2½ cups	Flour	591.5 ml
½ cup	Sugar	118.3 ml
1 cup	Margarine	236.6 ml
1 tbsp	Nutmeg	14.79 ml
2	Eggs	2
1 tbsp	Vanilla Extract	14.79 ml
2 tbsp	Cold Water	29.6 ml

Preheat oven to 350°F /180°C.

Spray pan with Cooking Spray. Melt margarine and mix in sugar, nutmeg, eggs, vanilla extract and cold water in a large bowl. Add half of flour and mix thoroughly. Add remaining flour and knead until it becomes a consistency of dough. Refrigerate for 15 minutes. On floured surface flatten dough by hand, cut with 9 inch/ 23 cm cookie cutter and place on cookie sheet; repeat process until all remaining dough is used. Bake for 30 minutes or until tea cakes are golden brown.

**After using the Prep Recipes in Chapter 4, resume the recipe at this point to complete the entrée.

Homemade Candy
(Servings 25 - 30)

Standard	Ingredients	Metric
2 cups	Condensed Milk	473.2 ml
2 cups	Sugar	473.2 ml
¾ cup	Margarine	188 ml
2 cups	Pecans (optional)	473.2 ml
	Cooking Spray	

Tip:
Use a non-stick sturdy pot with a long spoon.

Base a large cookie sheet with cooking spray and set aside. Place margarine, milk and sugar in large pot on medium-high heat. Stir ingredients constantly for 20 to 25 minutes until candy is caramel brown and while stirring moves as one solid unit. Test for readiness by dropping a small amount of candy in cold water to see if it is hard, crispy but not gooey. If harden, immediately remove from heat and mix in pecans and pour candy on cookie sheet and spread to desired thickness. Cut into squares, let stand for 5 minutes and serve.

Additional space for your family's favorite dessert recipes:

_____

_____

_____

_____

_____

_____

_____

_____

_____

_____

_____

_____

_____

_____

_____

_____

_____

_____

_____

_____

_____

_____

_____

_____

_____

_____

_____

_____

_____

_____

**After using the Prep Recipes in Chapter 4, resume the recipe at this point to complete the entrée.

9

Mama-Down-DA-Bayou

Favorite Recipes

Succotash
(Servings 10 - 12)

Standard	Ingredients	Metric
1 lb	Cut Corn	454 g
2 lbs	Raw Shrimp	907 g
1 ½ lb	Fresh Tomatoes	1
1 cup	Yellow Onion	236.6 ml
3	Cloves of Garlic	3
1 lb	Audoulle Sausage	454 g
1 pack	Dried Shrimp (small)	1 pack
3 lb	Cut Okra	1.4kg
1 lb	Butter Beans	g
1 cup	Oil	236.6 ml
	Cooking spray	
1 tsp	Creole Seasoning	4.93 ml
½ tsp	Cayenne Red Pepper (optional)	2.46 ml
3 cups	Shrimp Stock	590 ml

Peel and de-vein raw shrimp and set raw shrimp aside; place shrimp shells in large pot of water, boil for 30 minutes. Strain liquid from shrimp shells to create shrimp stock; discard shells and set shrimp stock aside. Preheat oil in a medium pot and fry okra for 15 minutes or until lightly brown. Drain oil from okra and set aside in strainer so remaining oil will drain from okra. Slice sausage and dice tomatoes and set aside. Dice yellow onion and garlic. Spray cooking spray in large pot and sauté garlic and yellow onion for 5 minutes or until tender. Add shrimp stock, corn, sausage, tomatoes, butter beans, Creole seasoning, cayenne red pepper and dry shrimp and cook for 20 minutes on medium heat. Add okra and shrimp and cook for another 10 minutes. Serve over cooked rice.

Fried Bread
(Servings 4)

Standard	Ingredients	Metric
3 cups	Self-rising Flour	0.7 l
1 cup	Water	236.6 ml
2 tbsp	Olive Oil	29.6 ml

Add 1 cup /236.6 ml of flour to water and mix thoroughly. Add another cup/236.6 ml of flour and knead until it becomes a consistency of dough. Add remaining flour until dough is no longer sticky. Flatten tennis ball size dough into a circular shape using rolling pin. Heat oil in medium sauce frying pan and place flatten dough in pan. Fry until bottom side of dough is a golden brown. Turn bread over and fry until golden brown. Remove from pan and place fried bread on plate lined with a paper towel. Continue above process to fry remaining dough. Serve with syrup, powered sugar, candied yams, peanut butter and jelly, cooked figs, blackberry dumplings or any of your favorite dessert toppings.

Core - to remove the inedible center of fruits and vegetables.

Appendix I - Calendars

Use the following calendars to help plan your special event.

Sunday	Monday	Tuesday	Wednesday	Thursday	Friday	Saturday

Sunday	Monday	Tuesday	Wednesday	Thursday	Friday	Saturday

Sunday	Monday	Tuesday	Wednesday	Thursday	Friday	Saturday

Sunday	Monday	Tuesday	Wednesday	Thursday	Friday	Saturday

Sunday	Monday	Tuesday	Wednesday	Thursday	Friday	Saturday

Sunday	Monday	Tuesday	Wednesday	Thursday	Friday	Saturda

Sunday	Monday	Tuesday	Wednesday	Thursday	Friday	Saturda

Appendix II: *Example of Pricing Table*

Event Dinner Menu Grocery List					
Gumbo	**Family 2**	90.00	**Cornbread Dressing**	**Family 4**	11.00
Gizzard	4 pk.		Corn meal	2 lbs	
Bologna	2 lbs		Flour	5 lbs	
Chicken Wings	2 lg pk.		Eggs		
Crabs	2 dz.		Raw Shrimp	2 lbs	
Raw Shrimp	6 lbs		Dried Shrimp	1 pk.	
Smoke Turkey Necks	2 lg pk.				
Smoke Sausage	1 box ea.				
Dried Shrimp	2 - 3 pk.				
Oysters	Small				
Okra	10 lbs				
Tripe	2 pk.				
Gravy	4 cans				
Ham	**Family 4**	12.00	**Potato Salad**	**Family 4**	8.00
Ham	Small		Potatoes	5 lbs	
brown Sugar	1 pk.		Eggs		
Slice Pineapple	1 Can		Mayo	Lg	
			Mustard		
			Relish		
			Sandwich Spread	Small Jar	

Baked Stewed Chicken	Family 4	10.00	Stewed Mirliton	Family 1	30.00
Wings, Legs &Thighs	2 lg pk.		Mirliton	18 count	
Seasonings			Raw Shrimp	3lbs	
Turkey	**Family 1**	10.00	**Mustard Greens**	**Family 3**	18.00
6lb Turkey			Mustard Greens	10 bunches	15.00
			Smoke Turkey Necks	1 pk	$3.00
Macaroni & Cheese	**Family 2**	10.00	**Sweet Peas**	**Family 4**	5.00
Margarine	2 sticks		Sweet Peas	1 big can	
Velveeta Cheese	1 lg box		Carrots	1 pk.	
Dry Cheese Packs	3 pk.				
Milk	4 cans & 1 qt/1 l				
Kraft mix Cheese	1 pk.				
Cheese Slice	1 pk.				

Dirty Rice	Family 1	20.00	Stewed Okra	Family 1	20.00
White Rice	15 lbs		Okra	6 lbs or 3 bags	
Brown Rice	2 lbs		Raw Shrimp	3 lbs	
Gravy	1 can		Sausage	1 pk.	
Turkey Ground.	1 pk.		Cayenne Red Pepper	1 bottle	
Ground. Beef	1 pk.		**Plastic ware**	Family 4	6.00
Cream of Mushroom Soup	1 can		Cups	1 pk.	
Cream of Chicken Soup	1 can		Plates	100 pk.	
Raw Turkey Sausage	1 pk.		Bowls	100 pk.	
Andouille	1 pk.		Napkins	100 pk.	
White Rice					
Stuffed Bell Peppers	Family 4	15.00	**Wheat Dinner Rolls**	Family 4	7.50
Green Bell Peppers					
Raw Shrimp	2 lbs				

Sweet Potato Pie	Family 1	4.00	Coconut Pie	Family 3	10.00
Sweet Potatoes	6 lbs		Coconut	2 lbs	
Sugar			Nut Meg		
Eggs			Milk		
Margarine			Cornstarch	1 bx	
Vanilla Extract	1 bottle		Cake Mix		
Cake Mix					
Yams	Family 1	6.50	Peach Cobbler	Family 1	5.00
Sweet Potatoes			Peaches	1 extra lg can	
Sugar-Free Brown Sugar	1 bag				
Sugar-Free White Sugar					
Margarine	1 pk. / box				
Pecan Pie	Family 3	25.00	Homemade Candy	Family 3	15.00
Pie crust	1 pk.		Condense Milk	8 cans	
Pecans			Sugar	10 lbs	
Honey			Margarine		
			Peanut Margarine		
			Pecans	1 pk.	

Bread Pudding	Family 4	10.00	**Strawberry Shortcake**	Family 4	3.50
Raisins	2 Boxes		Strawberries	1 Pk	
Crush pineapples	2 Cans		Whip cream	1 Container	
Bread	2 ea.				
Honey	1 Bottle				
Coconut	1 pk.				
Sugar/Sugar-Free					
Apple Pie	Family 4	2.50	**Rum Sauce**	Family 3	5.00
Upside Down Apple Pie	1				
Ice Cream	Family 4	5.00	**Drinks**	Family 3	24.00
Neapolitan	1 Gal/ 3.78 l		Sprite/Coke/ Orange/Red	36 cans	7.50
			Sparkling Flavor Water	24 bottles	12.00
			Daiquiri	1 bottle	5.00
			Assorted Kids Drinks	24 pk.	

Fill in the space provided below:

Third Meeting Date: __12/12/2008__ Time: 7 p.m.

Number of Families: ___4___

Event Grand Total: ___$388.00___

Each Family Contribution Amount: _$97.00_

Priority Item Due Date: __12/19/2008__

All Other Item Due Date: __12/24/2008__

Eve of the Event Dinner and Preparation:
Location: ___The Richardson's'___
Date: 12/24/2008 Time: _2 p.m._

Confirm Family Activities:

Confirm Event Date: _12/24/2008_ Time: __2 p.m.__

Next Meeting Date: 12/19/2008 Time: __7 p.m.__

Family 1 is ___The Richardson's___
Family 2 is ___The Whittington's___
Family 3 is ___The Scotts___
Family 4 is ___The Batistes___
Family 5 is _____
Family 6 is _____

Appendix III

Measurement Equivalents

<u>Dry</u>
3 tsp = 1 tbsp = ½ ounce
2 tbsp = 1/8 cup = 1 ounce
4 tbsp = ¼ cup = 2 ounces
5 1/3 tbsp = 1/3 cup= 2.6 ounces
8 tbsp = ½ cup = 4 ounces
12 tbsp = ¾ cup = 6 ounces
32 tbsp = 2 cups = 16 ounces

1 stick of butter = 8 tbsp = 4 oz = ¼ pound

<u>Liquid</u>
2 tbsp = 1 fluid ounce
¼ cup = 2 fluid ounces
½ cup = 4 fluid ounces = 8 tbsp
1 cup = 8 fluid ounces = 16 tbsp
1 ½ cup = 12 fluid ounces
2 cups = 16 fluid ounces = 1 pint
1 quart = 32 fluid ounces=2 pints=4 cups
1 gallon = 128 fluid ounces=4 quarts=8 pints

<u>Weight</u>
8 ounces = ½ pound
16 ounces = 1 pound
32 ounces = 2 pound
40 ounces = 2 ¼ pounds

Fry - to cook food in hot oil over moderate to high heat.

INDEX

MAMA-DOWN-DA-BAYOU

This was one word for us and our term of endearment for our maternal grandmother. She lived on a plantation but now they call it a farm. But back in the day we knew it as Belle Terre Plantation in the 1950's: with the main house at the front of the lane and a gravel road lined with row houses.

My grandmother cooked for the whole family that worked the sugar cane fields. The schedule was for the foreman, my step grandfather, who we called Old-man-tom, to get up at 4 am. He would ring the front bell tower which served as an alarm for everyone that worked the fields including their 3 daughters and 3 sons. In the meantime, Mama-down-da-bayou would prepare a hearty breakfast of fried bread, eggs, sausage and coffee. The water boy would come down the lane and retrieve breakfast from each household and bring the food along with water to the fields at 7 a.m. for each family member. My grandmother would then start to prepare for lunch from her garden; usually the meals would be red beans, white beans, cabbage, snap beans, okra or mustard greens served over rice. Everyone would come back in from the fields at 12:00 noon and eat lunch and return to the fields at 1:00 p.m. She would then start preparing supper usually choosing from her garden again from the same list mentioned above. The family would return from the fields one last time for the day at 5 p.m. The next day this ritual would start all over again.

What I mostly remember about my grandmother was while she prepared these daily meals she would be either praying or singing a hymn. And her essence for me will forever be unconditional eternal love. So I pray in some way this book is my love letter to her.

Your Loving Granddaughter,
Vera Richardson